Profile 8 – MAUD COTTER

Profile 8 – MAUD COTTER

Published as part of Gandon Editions'
PROFILES series on Irish artists (details p47).

ISBN 0946846 073

Editor   John O'Regan

Asst Editor   Nicola Dearey
Design   John O'Regan
                (© Gandon, 1998)
Production   Gandon
Photography   see list of illustrations, p43
Printing   Nicholson & Bass, Belfast

Distributed by Gandon and its overseas agents

GANDON EDITIONS
Oysterhaven, Kinsale, Co Cork
tel: +353 (0)21-770830 / fax: 770755

cover   *One Way of Containing Air*
                1997 (detail)

Publication grant-aided by
The Arts Council / An Chomhairle Ealaíon
and assisted by
Rubicon Gallery, Dublin

The Arts Council
An Chomhairle Ealaíon

Profile

Maud Cotter

GANDON EDITIONS

From Mouth to Air
1997, wax and pvc, 40 x 50 x 17 cm

The Voice of the Beehive

LUKE CLANCY

FOR HER 1998 DUBLIN SHOW, MAUD COTTER BUILT A WALL FIVE METRES WIDE BY THREE METRES high. It closed off nearly one-third of the Rubicon Gallery, a whitewashed space on the first floor of a Georgian building overlooking St Stephen's Green. Like all good walls, Cotter's seemed to invite destruction. In this case, however, the vulnerability of the slender vertical was not an illusion. Instead of being built of drystone or brick or plasterboard, this wall was made up of six panels of a honeycomb of steel and card, saturated with a microskin of white plaster. The touch of a finger, never mind the blow of a sledgehammer, would leave an unerasable imprint here. Even the soft light entering from the rear of the gallery passed through the structure, lending a faint glow to the mass of minute card triangles, as though what visitors looked on might be the head of an immense fibre-optic cable, a frenetic passageway rich with interlaced information, rather than an obstruction.

The work is very typical in the way it elaborates themes which have begun in recent times to animate the artist's work, themes related to Cotter's growing awareness of the interaction of social spaces – particularly those of the city – and the body. *In Absence*, the gleaming wall that lent its title to the exhibition, seems a kind of calling card for this dawning awareness. It offers a flickering image of a barrier, but

5

also intermittently of what is hidden. The wall may separate the body from its desire, from free movement, but it also offers an image of the body, an organisation of cells so intense that it gives rise to something else, something of which each individual cell can, by definition, not begin to contemplate. It is a model of the body as city and of the city as body.

In her essay 'Bodies-Cities', Elizabeth Grosz talks about the body as 'organically / biologically / naturally incomplete; it is indeterminate, amorphous, a series of uncoordinated potentialities which require social triggering, ordering and long-term "administration" regulated in each culture and epoch by what Foucault has called "the microtechnologies of power".' [1] How this administration functions, how it comes to constitute the body, and in turn the gendered body, relate not simply to culture and epoch, but to landscape and the social organisation produced by the interaction of the body and landscape. The body as constituted in terms of the city is not the same one constituted in other environments, and it is this realisation that has opened up a new area in Maud Cotter's mercurial practice.

For a large part of the 1990s, Cotter lived and worked in London. While the decision to leave Ireland was informed by several factors, the artist herself always sees the move in terms of what it has meant for her work. In London, Cotter worked at Delfina Studios, a multiple studio space that housed a large community of artists, and the place at which the accompanying interviews were conducted. Those who worked there ate together in a large refectory, a well ordered space that gave the whole building a focused sense of purpose.

If inside the studio had the serious calm of a workshop, outside in the small streets the atmosphere was akin to a busy hospital. Huge lengths of Bermondsey Street were lined with hoardings, pedestrians were guided into new, narrower routes by temporary railings and plastic tape. All around, the tin signs of contractors apologised for various inconveniences. Roads throughout the neighbourhood had been split and gutted, coils of fibre-optic cable lay waiting beside them, and there was the undeniable sense that the city was undergoing surgery of the most invasive kind. Traditional vessels, familiar flows could be sacrificed without fear; the new capillaries would without doubt out perform the old, leave no room for nostalgia.

In her studio, Cotter had been working on a wall-mounted piece. Two elongated forms in a sour, buttery colour were fixed to the studio wall about four feet from the ground. They might have been a pair of lungs. They were at least honeycombed with passages through which air might move, but they were now beyond use, at least for moving air.

The objects were, in fact, two small loaves of bread Cotter had take from the canteen and drenched in wax. Occasionally, Cotter's work is every bit as simple as that. At one time the artist had asked herself why her sculptures had to be so much work, why they had to involve the accrual of so much weighty matter over so many months. She says that this idea came into focus during the making of *Plateau* in 1994. The piece involved working with lengths of steel held together with bold, graphic welds, which came to form a bubbly, almost molten surface. These tiny details, moving like a swarm over the entire object, fostered a sense that immense forces were in the process of rupturing the fabric of the piece. But alongside this sensation of pressure of a tectonic order, *Plateau* also had a subtler, almost labial identity. Somewhere between these two senses of enfolding, the work sat heavily, squatting its space.

Successful in many ways, the work nevertheless struck Cotter as a failure of economy. The idea of cells, of repetition, of structures that arrive and exist through aggregation of minute, orchestrated parts is central to many strands of the artist's work, but after *Plateau*, Cotter began exploring alternative ways of representing these ideas. She sought alternatives that might offer similar visual possibilities to the heavyweight and more traditional media with which she had previously worked, but which would also allow her to close the enormous gaps that could open up between the artist and the completed work.

In her work, Cotter has often chosen to use materials such as steel and glass which might allow her to represent fluids, but with which struggle the battle to dominate the material must always mark the final work. In *The Heart Asks Pleasure*, for example, Cotter was able to make a foil of silver take on the appearance of a flowing, semeniferous substance.[2] But this kind of work must always operate through deception. The deception, the business of hiding one material behind the physicality of another, is, of course, near the heart of representation of all image-making. It can happen, nonetheless, that this game begins to become wearing, that the pleasure begins to wain.

Maud Cotter is exceptionally sensitive to the moment when this transformation takes place, to the spot when, for some reason connected with a topology we cannot readily perceive, a river seems to slow. Cotter ruthlessly finds the end of a body of work, and quietly slips into another, apparently untroubled with what this means in some grander picture of her art.

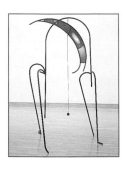

The artist who produced *Tempered* (1991) – a floor-standing frame of sinuous dark steel from which was suspended a Calder-esque crescent-shaped mobile, alarazin-coloured – ought to be quiet different from the one responsible for the two incarnations of *From Mouth to Air*, two pieces in which jaundiced wax is fixed to the wall, packed in a PVC wrapper. Just as the Cotter who emerged from the Crawford School of Art in 1978 and began exploring the medium of stained-glass (and was even identified by Nicola Gordon Bowe as a direct descendant of Evie Hone) is a very different artist from the one who in 1995 produced works such as the calamitous shrug of *Cliff*, these days there is another Cotter.

If there are links to be established between all these people, they are rarely enough to do with the physical presence of the sculptural objects. If when writing for the catalogue for Cotter's 1991 touring show, *My Tender Shell*, Nicola Gordon Brown could refer to continued evidence of the artist's 'deep fascina-tion with the ever-fluctuating Life Force, which governs all creative impulse...', it is be hard to be so unequivocal now.[3] For as the work moves through its spectrum of forms, it no longer seems possible that there is anything so unified, so monotonous as a single force which animates the work, unless of course that force is a force of transformation, of mutation, of disruption.

There is, of course, more than a journey towards more rapid sculptural expression behind Cotter's evolving forms.

Earlier in her career, Cotter's journey to Iceland had powerful effects on her work. She tends to explain the move as a desire to find a landscape that was somehow less worked over, need-ed less excavation, less disentanglement from the texts that had been written over it. Or as the poet John Montague wrote:

> Maud Cotter felt compelled to scrape her psyche clear by confronting the nude interior of Iceland, where the forces that make the earth still tremble the air, distort, shape and thrust the crust of the emerging earth. It is this journey into an always shifting interior, this persis-tent pagan restlessness mixing sky and earth, which has inspired her latest work, and will continue to underlie it, the primordial disputing our more settled realm, bub-bling chaos against the calmer legacy of a centre of cul-ture like Chartres.[4]

Could those kinds of attitudes, those kinds of desires, ever be reconciled with working in an urban environment, in a place where the sense of an unwritten world should be absent? The answer has to do with how closely you look. The pilgrimage is always a subjective journey. The centre of belief is pretty much where you conceive it to be. So if it is simply possible to meet materials with this idea in mind, anything may be possible.

If one sculptor may find the narrative flattened into isthmus rock conducive, another may find that man-made materials might have an unexpected story to tell. It may seem an extrava-gant claim, but Cotter is the only artist I can think of who has this particular relationship to her material. Others sculptors may like to call in the psychic energy of ancient limestone when dealing with the urban landscape, but Cotter has travelled down a path which sees her uncovering the same energies in synthetic material. It is as though as fossils of ancient existence might crop up in stone, so the spoor of our own may show up in the raw materials we invent. Could the light that passes through a sheet of PVC be so different to that entering Chartres cathedral through the rose window? Something with which we are faced daily may also be, paradoxically, an unexplored place, an untouched set of ideas. The only way to find out is to dismiss familiar values and experiment. This dismissal is a constant feature in Cotter's work.

Even so, the artist's journey has, interestingly and productively, not been a journey towards ever greater notions of essence, or purity and rare refinement. Quite the opposite in fact. Cotter maintains a powerful interest in landscape, but her work has more and more begun to frame landscape in terms of the forces that police our perception of it. Her work has, for many years, explored landscape as both a metaphor for and an extension of the body. What she has achieved recently, however, is to switch her attention away from the depopulated landscapes of Ireland or Iceland towards the urban environment.

Cotter is an uncommon artist in that she has achieved a type of celebration of the urban environment that is neither utopian nor sentimental nor ironic. By examining plastic or polymers, she seems able to give the sort of reading a geologist might with a core sample. What might only be visible in the layers of compressed dust, dirt and stone, Cotter has begun to find in substances such as corrugated paper. The artist sees this development as contiguous with work that she had previously made, work in which she began to feel out a connection between the body and landscape. As she says in the accompanying interview: 'I feel in contact with the fabric of things, not the narrative. I inhabit this new world now in a way that I used to inhabit landscape...'

The difference in her work is that now, rather than seeking out a space in which to recreate or to recover a broken relationship with the landscape, Cotter is uncovering a new one. It is making visible, in a way that is palpably optimistic, that a sense of alienation is not a pre-given in city life. If, as Cotter's work now seems to suggest, there are very real connections between the body and the urban landscape and the minutiae of the urban landscape, then it may be possible to make art about urban experience that moves beyond the ironic buckshot to what amounts to a spiritual relationship with the technological environment. The work that achieves this is quiet and still, but undeniably anxious, tightly structured but with a sense of organic, stochastic development rather than of rigid planning.

Italian manufactured tri-wall card appeared several times in the work in Cotter's recent Rubicon show, most grandly in *In Absence* – the artist's own building site project – but also notably in a far smaller, ostensibly more modest form in *Mundus*, a low, tapered septagon, comprised of layer upon layer of corrugated cardboard punctured at its apex by a small ocular opening, calling to mind the Pantheon, the great navel of Hadrian's Rome. Cotter makes reference to the 'hell hole' traditionally dug to mark the beginning of a Roman city. But where a mundus in ancient Rome may have, according to Richard Sennett,[5] been the point where the Romans thought the city was connected to the gods interred in the earth and the gods of light in the sky, Cotter's *Mundus* always seems to undermine any sense of a power superior to that expressed in the honeycomb of little spaces that the card creates. This mundus exists because of the life that forms around it, rather than the other way around.

In *The Eye of the City*, Cotter moves into the territory of museums, methods of investigation and categorisation. Akin to many of the works in Cotter's Rubicon show, the piece uses small cells of card as its basic unit, again multiplying to reach a sort of critical mass. Small square sections of thin, sharply cut corrugated card are layered into a tall, slender stack, held together by a synthetic microcrystalline wax. The miniature building is then placed inside a specially cast bell jar, as though it were a specimen of a hive created by a swarm of high-modernist bees. The suggestion of bees (which the artist prefers not to emphasise) helps to underline a sense that the piece is as much a rich set of relationships, a coded integration of individuals, a network, as it is a stand-alone structure. Scale in the piece always seems under stress, as the elements that support integrity struggled with those that point to the individuality of each tiny unit. All of this is presented, through the bell jar, as a scientific specimen, a finished judgement about what is the master form of this object. But the work constantly slips away from offering even the most elliptical of facts, providing if anything a darkly humorous homily on the crumbling architectures of knowledge, a reading that is helped by the disarmingly miniaturised scale of the work.

One Way of Containing Air performs a similar feat of disorientation. The human-scaled sculpture stands on the floor, but suggests a structure that should not be contained by the gallery space. Instead it seems as though the work itself might, somewhere at the core of its intense networked structured, play home to a hundred galleries. One again, the structure is built of corrugated card, but here the three-dimensionality of the piece encourages an even more focussed notion of a model of social space, of physical integration. But once more, this is balanced with a sense of discrete cells finally reaching a potential. Like an artist's body of work in which pieces gradually move together, not always at the same speed or in the same direction, but always for the same reason. Works are finding each other constantly, until they achieve a critical mass and they begin to mean, to have the power to say things together that were always just beyond their grasp when they stood alone. And though this is a cruder statement of what is at stake than one might ever find in the work, this does seem to be the territory that Maud Cotter has begun to explore.

Luke Clancy is a writer and critic based in Dublin. He writes on Irish culture for the *Irish Times*.

Footnotes

[1] Elizabeth Grosz, 'Bodies-Cities', *Sexuality and Space*, ed. Beatriz Colomina (Princeton Architectural Press, 1992)
[2] In the case of *The Heart Asks Pleasure*, the deception was effective. The suggestion that the flowing shape into which the silver had been worked was a matter of gravity worked rather too well. The work was destroyed when, following an exhibition in Europe, the silver leaf was rolled up and packed alongside the rigid elements of the work.
[3] *Maud Cotter – My Tender Shell*, essay by Nicola Gordon Bowe, intro by John Montague (Gandon Editions, 1991)
[4] ibid.
[5] Richard Sennett, *Flesh and Stone* (WW Norton, New York, 1994)

A Conversation with the Artist

LUKE CLANCY

Luke Clancy – For many years, steel and glass have been signature materials of your work. When did your interest in using these substances begin?

Maud Cotter – As a younger woman I needed something like steel. There was a flintiness and an anger in me that only steel could satisfy. I was introduced to steel by John Burke. Steel to me was more like a piece of meat than a hard industrial material – you heated it and it expanded, it flaked when forged, and it groaned when you put it into cold water. It was very organic, like flesh really. I liked the range of usage and the range of softness and hardness that it offered. You could allow it to be heavy and fleshy, but you could then grind it or file it. There is this incredible range of handling in the material and I liked that. This is the approach I brought to glass. Glass has that sort of volatility, that live element of steel that I was connecting with – the liquidity, the hardness, but also the ability for it to be quite a mercurial medium and have an aptitude for change.

I assume there's a sort of affinity between the materials you use and the issues with which you want to deal, so I wonder to what extent, say, your interest in steel as a material leads you toward a certain territory?

11

Well, to be honest, materials are not my first consideration. Obviously the relationship between the materials and the concept is a complex one, but I would see myself as more conceptually driven. It was quite a surprise to me that I became involved in glass, but I was concerned with finding out some thing that glass, in particular, made possible. I've always tried to retain a degree of ruthlessness about my interests. The material serves my investigation into what my mind is projecting. The materials are very much a means to an end. In some instances I worked with what I had to hand, and I think that the current work has been characterised by a kind of opening, an involvement in a wider range of materials.

For one part of your work the topography of Iceland was very important. How did you become interested in that? It seems to be something that has influence right into the present work.

I started off connecting with the Atlantic edges of Ireland and the wildness of that terrain. I had a sense of an undisturbed presence there that hadn't really been tamed in the same way as, say, European landscapes which had an extensive history of habitation. I became more involved in land as a reservoir for human energy. I see energies in landscape, and that was what I was pursuing. I always saw work as a means through which you could pack energy into material. It came to a point where I felt it was the intricacy and narratives of Irish landscape that were holding me back. I felt completely overcomplicated by it. Now, I don't know whether I had worked myself into a state exploring every aspect of the particular goldfish bowl I was in, or whether in fact – and I suspect it's the case – it was too rich for me. I needed something harder, something more confrontational. Then I discovered the Icelandic terrain.

You have said that the landscape there allowed you to conceptualise, in some way, the body. How did this come about?

I think eventually that is what happened when I confronted that landscape, having to find some sort of level of dialogue or co-existence. It eventually emerged through my sense of the body in the landscape. I began to identify with the volcanoes in terms of their chambers or mouths, or the openings in the terrain that spat and gurgled and almost seemed to be saying something, throwing these lacy films of calcium, and weaving these extra-ordinary latticed deposits. I was, in a way, identifying with these things ·in terms of skin, and I felt them so strongly that they induced a sense of connectedness with my body. It's not something I would take too seriously, I just think that's my sensory connection... But there is that kind of body connection intrinsic to my work, I suppose. How do you find what's true for you to do? How do you find it? My train of knowing is through what my body chooses, a form of psychic and physical recognition, and it is also guided by my need, but if it doesn't connect with me in a physical sense, then it's dead for me.

The approach you're describing involves some precognitive sense, something before an intellectual sense, and that's a bit...

You find it a bit dodgy? Well, I'm full of suspicion, of course. I mean, there's nothing ever set except that I am very interested in consciousness and partial consciousness. Being able to take that very, very tentative element and bring that into a physical state while retaining that very fine connection is what I have found hardest to do. The piece *Plateau* epitomises that part of my work. But for some reason being some sort of sculptural gymnast didn't really satisfy me. I wanted to get down into the underlayers and bring the small little inarticulate things out.

It seems to me that moving to London represented a shift in your practice towards something more linguistic. Because the city is mapped out through the literature of the Romantics, you are faced with a linguistic construction.

The reasons for my coming to London in 1991 were, to a degree, circumstantial and personal. I was in a transitional phase, around the time of the *My Tender Shell* touring show. I needed to move on in my work, and leaving Ireland was one way of doing that. I don't see London exclusively in the constructed or fabricated way that you suggest. I recognise that it has the imprint of centuries of conscious human activity on it, and I enjoy the scale and depth of that, but the city, for me is as much a seething growth as mapped, but I can accept that my work has become more overtly conceptual.

What I've been doing since I came to London is just inhabiting that territory more fully, and I think it's getting more refined and defined, and when I use this up, then I'm going to have to start again. Sometimes I draw myself into new conceptual terrains and then by creating an environment of drawings, I can make objects that inhabit that territory, if you like. So I always see new movements in my work as being different territories.

At what point did you move away from the drawings back towards sculpture? Because obviously you must reach a cut-off point where you feel, 'Well this is the space, now let's go in.'

I think it comes to a point where in some way I get lonely – I just really want to have things in my studio, like I just love the company of my sculptures. They're rather like creating people that are in your life, and at the same time I don't really mind when they leave. So, I began to make these pieces that were modelled with quarter-inch steel bar. I wanted an incredibly dense and compact form, and I found myself combining glass with steel in a way that, in some instances, used the glass as a sort of bodily fluid. There's one piece called *Aboriginal Ice*, which was one I learned a lot from. I was very interested in getting a sense of urban liquid that wasn't sea or fresh water, that had no sense of a bodily fluid but had a sense of seeping out. I always feel that in cities, the water and the bad drainage create a feeling of slow seepage and this use of glass became a way of articulating a sense or a feeling that I had.

Yeats has described the aesthetic source as being an 'Aboriginal Ice'. I always thought this a very sprightly way of describing it, this fresh spring, inspiring water. I didn't really feel that this existed for me any more. I felt it was more of a stagnant sea, an insipid seeping. So, it was one of those pieces where I felt myself connecting, in a different way. Connecting with nature, but also with what was very much an urban sensibility. I think through the work there had emerged this urban-ness. There were other pieces I did around that time. One was *Broken Vowel,* and again it used the notion of liquidity and the notion of mouth. Then there was *Ope,* a very simple little piece; it had a mouthpiece and it was sitting on a piece of glass that was pouring off the shelf. The piece was concerned with the idea of

separation, where the liquid would never be part of that orifice. The relationship between mouth and liquid had become irretrievably severed. A distance, or a space began to come between elements in my work and separate them.

Sometimes the sculptures seem to explain why you are not going to continue working in a particular vein, whereas in fact they are the beginning of a particular way of working.

I think what's happening is that every piece you make is a reason not to make that again. Every niche you find is somewhere you could never be again, so there's a constant sense to me of lamenting – loss of self and exploring even more fractured parts of self. If you were to dwell in those happy terrains that you know and inhabit, then you'd stagnate, and so you've no choice. You've no choice but to leave everything.

Still, you don't at all model them as a 'healing'. They are just an identification of that gap. They don't help?

Oh, they do, yeah. That's about the only thing that does help – the actual making. I think that names something not previously named. Once you name something you can then move on.

You seem not simply to move on; you seem to become almost disgusted with something once you've named it.

Not disgusted, not disgusted, no, no. Sometimes you don't really know things you make until maybe a year later, so there isn't a fixed narrative. It's all moving together as a stream. I might work on four or five pieces together, so I'm carried very much in that stream. As I go on, I know parts of it but I never know the full thing until I come to the end, and I never really get there.

Do you think that your work has become more social since you moved to London?

I am very concerned with masses of people that have no voice. I'm concerned with the lack of access that human potential has despite the sophistication, technical sophistication of our era. I think there is a loss. There is a loss of innate connectedness with nature and with self that I'm very concerned about. In that sense, yes, it is political, because it is saying, 'Remember me, I'm part of your body and being. I'm a very fine sense, a very fine filament which tied you to the world.' It's about identity in that sense, and then about finding a way of being your integral self in the face of environmental pressure, political stress and all these things that corrode. In a way I think of my heavy sculptural work as warriors combating this, whereas now I see the new work as rather like a knife that gets under a layer and is just teasing out those layers of encrustation, of falseness, of materialism. They are little bits of things which can implant and quietly change the way people see things.

There is a strong tradition in the Romantics of seeing London as offering a particularly vivid flashpoint in the advance of industrial society, of the subjugation of a different set of values. Have those kind of ideas had an impact on you?

I suppose that there was a rough model of that in my leaving Ireland. The Irish landscape fed my work and then adjusting to the intensity of the built environment in a place like London, I felt myself choked with the loss of being in contact with nature and the ease of people in Ireland. All the work I have done here has been about that separation. Of course the dialogue with Ireland never stops; I travel back and forth a lot.

Seeing London through Blake's eyes helped me to work here at first, until I built my own aesthetic territory. *Leaf II* is a piece influenced by a William Blake drawing titled *What is Man?*. The drawing depicts a worm on a leaf – a piece of organic matter on a horizontal plane. I was attracted to such a fundamental question being asked with two elements in an uncomplicated formal relationship. It is a corner piece of galvanised steel grounded by the weight of a section of compressed copper pipes. The fact that it is pinned to the ground by weight is important. It's like this symbol of human physicality and presence fitted into a corner.

How would you characterise your interest in public art?

I am interested in it to the extent that connection is important

to me; sensory connection to the built environment is very much part of my work at the moment. This concern has arisen from the general sense of displacement I felt on leaving Ireland and the crisis of meaning in my work, changing from landscape as a primary force to the city as fabric and its connection to the mind and body.

Richard Sennett talks about the visceral connection of place in his book *Flesh and Stone*, which helped me understand my relationship with Ireland. He goes on to discuss the natural lack of connection in a large city where one is say, travelling in the underground, moving and not committing to objects one sees or places one is passing through. This feeling of being processed by the city is interesting in relation to public art. Though it's not always the case, it poses a question. How do you build sensory connection in a city? What form should public art take? I feel the need to make a more intrinsic connection.

Once you understand that this context of weak commitment is the one in which you are working, then you must respond to that. You need to do something that connects very deeply with the fabric, environmentally and socially, so that it will resonate in that context and so that it will bind in some way, create strands which do give a sense of place and connection.

Artists invariably complain that their work is used as a cosmetic dressing. Sometimes you find that building interiors, never mind building exteriors, are very triumphal and self-fulfilled – lots of panelling and fixtures inside and an impenetrable skin outside – which can make it very difficult to make a mature aesthetic intervention. There is no door left open, only minor gaps.

How would you relate that notion that there is often nothing that an artist can really do if the architect works in a certain manner to your own experiences of public art commissions?

Well, in the case of the piece I made for the Green Building in Temple Bar, I was offered a period of consultation with the architect. The piece would not have been as it is except for the fact that there was dialogue, which I found stimulating. Its level of intervention has become meshed into the fabric of the building. I like that feeling of the piece becoming very connected with the building. It is a door, a window and a letterbox as well as being a piece in itself.

So is that your preferred model for a public art project, integrating your work with somebody else's work?

That is certainly one avenue, but the extraordinary thing about the whole area is that there are more and more ways of making art in that context. There are temporary artworks, which can have more of an effect, become more of a mental event, because of their transitory nature. The absence of Rachel Whiteread's *House* is even more stimulating than when it was there! If you walk out the door, how energising is it to walk down your footpath, to stand and wait for a bus? How does your environment connect with you? How does it make you feel? I would like to think public art is about creating an environment that makes that kind of stimulating connection with your body and your mind. That in a way is what art is about, raising levels of perception, creating points of connection. Conceptually, anything I would have to offer would come from the studio work. Keeping that critical is very important to me.

In your work, there seems to be a dialogue about whether labour should be important. In the larger pieces, like Plateau, *the labour is huge and it is almost an industrial process. In other pieces it is really compressed, heading toward invisibility.*

Yes, *Plateau* was as strange in terms of labour because I was doing it myself, and it was so tedious and so slow that I felt the speed of the process was inhibiting the fluency of decision. When I got somebody to help me, I got it done faster. It needed that drive and fluency and energy to complete itself. Later, I was looking at *Plateau* and wondering, 'Why can't I just throw it at the wall? Why do I have to labour so hard? Why am I like an archaeologist?' I just thought that it was a personality compulsion. I wanted to try and break out of my own compulsive attraction to toil – it seems so primitive.

So I did *Cliff*. It's an angle-iron with a piece of glass just floating – you can see where the glass is connected. This piece is like *Leaf II* in ways. It is intestinal, it has a feeling of matter, you know, of human body. I called it *Cliff* because the sculptural relationships were only barely connecting enough to be a piece. The point of connection of the sculptural relationships was on the edge of nothingness, on the edge of not being a piece: so fine that it was reduced to the fundamental attraction of materials. I felt that if you reduced the relationships further to a finer point of focus then it would become stunningly real. If you could make elements just be together, they would acquire a resonance which, to me, is very much about what it's like to be living in the 20th century. In the recent work, it's like time has become more compressed, telescoped a little, whereas my earlier pieces once inhabited time in a lavish way. Now it's more lucid, less physical, and I think London has done that to me.

When it came to making Shroud, *did you decide that you could achieve similar things without putting the physical elements together?*

I found this quite peculiar. *Shroud* was very odd for me because it was about the air inside. This is the first time I used a cage but the piece is not about the cage. The object wasn't important to me, it was the fact that the air was held inside. I drew the cloud element in Australia and I couldn't throw it out. It hovered, I mean I put it up in my studio and there would be this little cloud hovering around, so to speak. I couldn't get rid of it and eventually it was like a question mark. I began to work with the questions that this pursuit posed me. That is how the cage section became a chamber of air.

It is very interesting that a model of the body seems to work better if it's disintegrated. Do you ever look upon it as an anthropomorphic piece?

Yes, because it is a funerary piece. When I wrapped the lower section in finely woven copper mesh, I felt like I was wrapping a piece of a body that had died nameless and never achieved any certainty. While making the piece I was concerned that the cage didn't offer the lower section a protective covering. To maintain the vulnerability of the piece it was necessary to eternally separate the elements.

Would it be true to say that you've become more interested in what's happening in the space between the various components of the work, in opening up those spaces?

Yes, it's like everything else. I found myself going back and forward – it's like I move ahead two steps and move back one.

You have come all the way from using steel and iron to making intensely vulnerable pieces from more delicate materials. Do you see the models of social and physical organisation that you once saw in landscape offered now by these materials? Do we somehow reflect and inflect the materials we create and use?

Well, yes. Reflect and inflect make sense to me, almost like a process of breathing in the city physically, viscerally and intellectually. I think that intimacy with the structures around me was what deepened my connection with what was literally on the studio floor. I felt myself moving towards a molecular vision, rather than a physical form. The card pieces evolved from being in the company of this little piece of card I found in my studio. I used the PVC to covered my pieces to protect them from dust and loved the world that created. So my choices were informed by the intensity of the present. The wall-piece made for the Rubicon show was a metaphor for that process, body as a filter of the city. The chambers of air on either side of that piece were important to me. I found that piece very rewarding as I wanted to find something that encompassed the monumental and the molecular, form and filter. I titled it *In Absence* before I made it in the hope that it would gesture to that sensitivity of being with materials in the present moment, but dispersed as well, almost dematerialised, dispersing the connection.

The *In Absence* show for me has been a resolution, an arrival into cohabitation with the structures we build around our bodies. I feel in contact with the fabric of things, not the narrative. I inhabit this new world now in a way that I used to inhabit landscape. I feel indivisible from it.

[interviewed in London, 1997]

Rev Michael Scott Memorial Window
1988-89, stained glass, 183 x 46 cm (detail)
St Pancras Church, Kingston, Lewes, East Sussex

Djinn
1990, steel and glass, 173 x 25 x 21 cm

opposite
Burning Heart
1990, stained glass, 66 x 71 cm

Pool
1993, steel and glass, 46 x 27 x 29 cm

Mouth
1994, copper, steel and glass, 18 x 50 x 23 cm

In the Palm of My Hand
1993, copper, steel and glass
66 x 35 x 35 cm

Cave
1991-94, steel, 277 x 60 x 31 cm

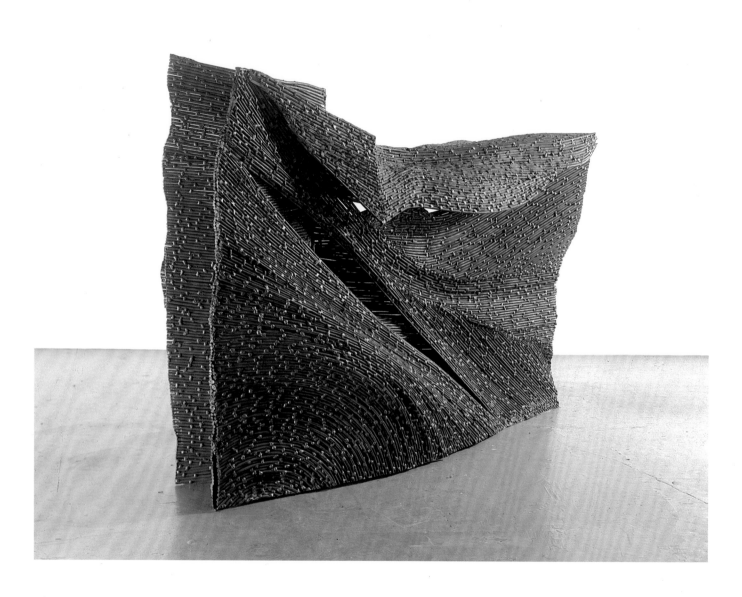

Plateau
1994, steel, 94 x 131 x 44 cm
Profil Arbed Collection, Luxembourg

Face
1990, drawing, 113 x 78 cm

Absolute Jellies Make Singing Sounds
1994, steel, glass, perspex, copper and lead
600 x 250 x 30 cm
The Green Building, Temple Bar, Dublin

Cliff
1995, glass, steel and copper, 50 x 125 x 24 cm

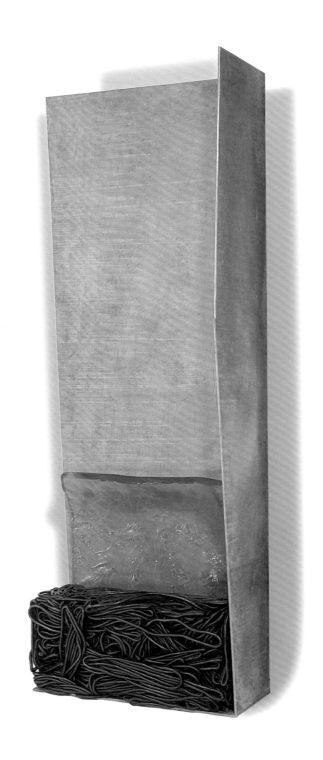

Leaf II
1994-95, steel, glass and copper
141 x 58 x 31 cm

30
Shroud
1994-95, steel, copper and paper, 115 x 30 x 20 cm

opposite
Cage
1996, steel, cement, PVC and latex, 300 x 180 x 180 cm

In the grace of its own shadow
1994, stone, lead, PVC and steel, 228 x 82 x 35 cm
Irish Museum of Modern Art, Dublin

opposite
Flying High Feeling Low
1996, copper and steel, 38 x 17 x 50 cm

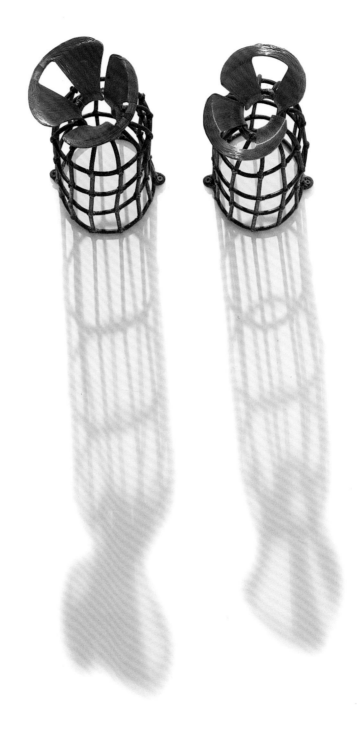

Eating Air after Dark
1997, glass, plaster, wax, latex and silicon
161 x 82 x 14 cm

opposite
One Way of Containing Air
1997, card, 202 x 76 x 31 cm
Irish Museum of Modern Art, Dublin

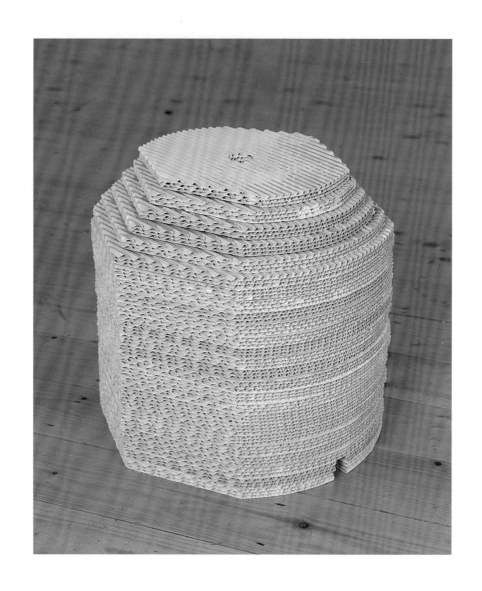

Mundus
1997, card and plaster, 37 x 36 x 38 cm

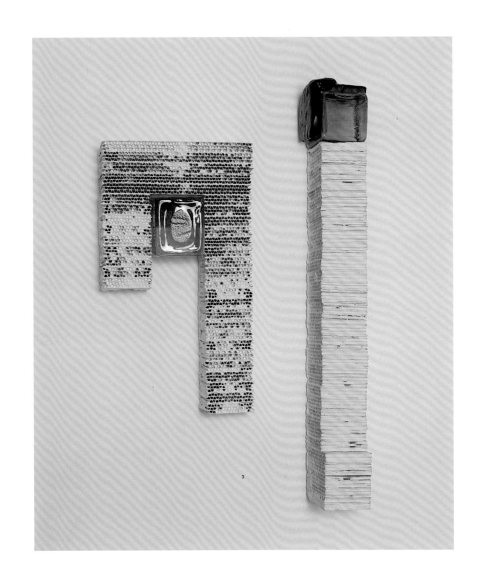

A Place To Be (I, II)
1997, glass, plaster, card and wood, 65 x 10 x 12 cm

In Absence
1998, card, plaster and steel, 490 x 290 x 3 cm

In Absence
1998, installation at Rubicon Gallery, Dublin

Breath
1997, wax and PVC, 187 x 128 x 30 cm

Aboriginal Ice
1993-94, steel and glass, 42 x 128 x 24 cm

LIST OF ILLUSTRATIONS

RH = Ronnie Hughes / CL = Chris Leinhart / DM = Denis Mortell / JS = John Searle

Aidan O'Shea

MAUD COTTER

1954	Born in Wexford
1972-78	Crawford College of Art and Design, Cork
1989	Co-founder, National Sculpture Factory Cork (director since 1989)
1992-97	Delfina Studios, London
	Lives and works in Cork

Solo Exhibitions

1998	*In Absence*, Rubicon Gallery, Dublin
1996	*Outer Veil, Inner Shroud*, Economist Plaza, St James's, London
1995	*Mute Displacement*, Galerie Schlossgoart, Luxembourg
	The Heart Asks Pleasure, Rubicon Gallery, Dublin
1991-92	*My Tender Shell*, Triskel Arts Centre, Cork; Maison Internationale de Rennes, France; West Wharf Gallery, Cardiff
1991	Riverrun Gallery, Dublin
1983	*Stained Glass, Painting and Drawing*, Crawford Municipal Art Gallery, Cork

Commissions

1998	*Place*, Mahon, Cork (fabricated brass in integrated garden), Cork Corporation
1994	*Absolute Jellies Make Singing Sounds*, The Green Building, Temple Bar, Dublin (entrance incorporating glass wall filled with recycled materials), Murray O'Laoire Architects / Temple Bar Properties
	Michael Scott Memorial Window, St Pancras Church, Kingston, Lewes, East Sussex (stained glass window), Hon. David Astor
	Fast Fish Loose Fish, Castlebar Library, Co Mayo

(steel and glass mobile), Mayo County Council
Hybrid, Ballyroan Library, Co Dublin (steel, glass and perspex mobile), Dublin County Council
That Sound Meets Sense, Straight As Lemons Meet Fish, Dublin Castle (stained glass window), OPW

1985   *Route Impeller*, Triskel Arts Centre, Cork (stained glass window), New Ireland Assurance

Selected Group Exhibitions

1998   *A Collection in the Making*, IMMA, Dublin
        25 Years of Kilkenny Arts Week, Butler Gallery, Kilkenny
1997   Artists in Residence, Lonschthaus beim Engel, Luxembourg
        Human Nature – Seven Artists from Ireland, touring Newfoundland
1996   Eighth Mostyn Open Exhibition, Oriel Mostyn Gallery, Llandudno
        Five Sculptors, Butler House, Kilkenny
        Proem, Rubicon Gallery, Dublin
1995   *Compulsive Objects*, Rubicon Gallery, Dublin (curator)
        10, Galerie Schlossgoart, Luxembourg
        Irish Steel, Model Arts Centre, Sligo; Limerick City Gallery of Art; Crawford Municipal Art Gallery, Cork
1994   Delfina Studios, London (also 1993)
        Siolrú, RHA Gallagher Gallery, Dublin
1993   *Neon-Glas-Licht*, Galerie Monica Borgward, Bremen
1991   *Ice in our Luggage*, Swansea Arts Workshop
        Espace, RHA Gallagher Gallery, Dublin
1990   City Arts Centre, Oklahoma City
1989-90 National Self-Portrait Collection, touring Ireland
1989   *Stefnumot a Islandi*, Nordic House, Reykjavik
        International Stained Glass Exhibition, Chartres
        36 Frauen aus 12 Landern, touring Germany
1987   *20th Century Irish Art*, AIB Collection, Dublin
        SADE, Crawford Municipal Art Gallery, Cork
1986   *Cork Glass Art* (Arts Council touring show), London, Belfast, Galway, Limerick, Dublin

1985   *CAN – Cork Art Now*, Crawford Gallery, Cork
1984   Independent Artists, Guinness Hop Store, Dublin
1982   GPA Awards for Emerging Artists, Douglas Hyde Gallery, Dublin

Selected Bibliography

1996   *Human Nature,* essay by Bonnie Leyton (British Council, Belfast)
1995   *Irish Steel*, essay by Mark Ewart (Gandon Editions)
        Maud Cotter – Mute Displacement, essay by Janice West (Galerie Schlossgoart, Luxembourg)
1993   *Neon-Glas-Licht*, essay by Rudi Stem (Galerie Monica Borgward, Bremen)
1992   *Women's Art at Newhall*, essay by Marina Warner (Newhall, Cambridge)
1991   *Maud Cotter – My Tender Shell*, essay by Nicola Gordon Bowe, intro by John Montague (Gandon)
        'Black Rivers Bite Deep' by Maud Cotter, *Stet* (Cork)
1986   *Cork Glass Art*, essay by Nicola Gordon Bowe (Triskel Arts Centre, Cork)
1983   *20th Century Irish Stained Glass*, essay by Nicola Gordon Bowe (Arts Council, Dublin)
        Stained Glass, Painting and Drawing, essay by Nicola Gordon Bowe (Crawford Gallery, Cork)

Collections – Arts Council / An Chomhairle Ealaíon; AIB Bank; Crawford Municipal Art Gallery, Cork; Delfina Studios, London; Dublin Castle; GPA; Irish Museum of Modern Art, Dublin; National Self-Portrait Collection of Ireland; New Hall College, Cambridge; Nishida Art Museum, Kamiichi, Japan; Office of Public Works; Profil Arbed Collection, Luxembourg; University College Cork; private collections in Ireland, Germany, Luxembourg, Iceland, UK, USA

Maud Cotter is represented by the Rubicon Gallery
10 St Stephen's Green, Dublin 2
(tel 01-6708055 / fax 01-6708057 / e-mail rubi@iol.ie)

GANDON EDITIONS

Gandon Editions is the foremost producer of books on Irish art and architecture.

Gandon Editions was established in 1983 and was named after the architect James Gandon (1743-1823), as the initial focus was on architecture titles.

We now produce 20 to 25 art and architecture titles per year, both under the Gandon imprint and on behalf of a wide range of art and architectural institutions in Ireland. We have produced over 180 titles to date.

Gandon books are available from good bookshops in Ireland and abroad, or direct from:

GANDON EDITIONS
Oysterhaven, Kinsale, Co Cork
tel: +353 (0)21 770830 / fax: 770755

PROFILES

In 1996, Gandon Editions launched PROFILES – a series of medium-format books on contemporary Irish art. In 1997, we launched a companion series on Irish architecture. Both series are edited by John O'Regan.

Each volume in the series carries two major texts – an essay and an interview with the artist / architect – and is heavily illustrated in colour. They are of a standard design and pagination, with 48 pages in a 23 cm square format, and retail at £7.50 paperback.

already published

Profile 1 – PAULINE FLYNN
essays by Paul M O'Reilly and Gus Gibney
ISBN 0946641 722   Gandon Editions, 1996

Profile 2 – SEÁN McSWEENEY
essay by Brian Fallon
interview by Aidan Dunne
ISBN 0946641 617   Gandon Editions, 1996

Profile 3 – EILÍS O'CONNELL
essay by Caoimhín Mac Giolla Léith
interview by Medb Ruane
ISBN 0946641 870   Gandon Editions, 1997

Profile 4 – SIOBÁN PIERCY
essay by Aidan Dunne
interview by Vera Ryan
ISBN 0946641 900   Gandon Editions, 1997

Profile 5 – MARY LOHAN
essay by Noel Sheridan
intro and interview by Aidan Dunne
ISBN 0946641 889   Gandon Editions, 1998

Profile 6 – ALICE MAHER
essay by Medb Ruane
interview by Medb Ruane
ISBN 0946641 935   Gandon Editions, 1998

Profile 7 – CHARLES HARPER
essay by Gerry Walker
interview by Aidan Dunne
ISBN 0946846 111   Gandon Editions, 1998

Profile 8 – MAUD COTTER
essay by Luke Clancy
interview by Luke Clancy
ISBN 0946846 073   Gandon Editions, 1998

Profile 9 – MICHEAL FARRELL
essay by Aidan Dunne
intro and interview by Gerry Walker
ISBN 0946846 138   Gandon Editions, 1998

titles in preparation

CECILY BRENNAN
BARRIE COOKE
FELIM EGAN
VIVIENNE ROCHE
NIGEL ROLFE

to be continued ...